Quick Revision

KS3

French

Caroline Woods

First published 2007
exclusively for WHSmith by
Hodder Education, an Hachette UK company
338 Euston Road
London
NW1 3BH

Impression number 10 9 8 7 6 5 4
Year   2011

A CIP record for this book is available from the British Library.

The right of Caroline Woods to be identified as the author of this work has been asserted by her.

Cover illustration by Sally Newton Illustrations.

Typeset by Starfish Design Editorial and Project Management Ltd.
ISBN: 978 0 340 94311 3

Printed and bound in the UK by Hobbs the Printers Ltd.

Accents

Here are the most common kinds of accents.

Acute accent – over an **e**. This is a really important accent on verbs. In the perfect tense, it appears on the last **e** of **er** verbs, e.g. **joué**. Without it, the meaning of what you say can become confused. Think of an acute angle (⟋) to get the accent in the right direction – **é**! It sounds like the *a* in the word *hay*.

Circumflex accents appear over any given vowel, e.g. **hôtel**. (A circumflex shows that in old French spelling there used to be an **s** after the **o**.)

Cedilla – this goes under the letter **c** to soften it if the **c** is followed by **a**, **o** or **u**. (e.g. **ça**, **garçon**). It sounds like an English **s**.

Grave – this accent also goes over an **e**, (e.g. **frère**, where it makes a sound like *e* in the word *edge*) and in words like **à** (*to*) and **où** (*where*).

Adjectives

An adjective is a describing word. It describes a noun. *Big, little, funny* and *red* are all adjectives. In French, most adjectives go after the noun. Adjectives agree with the noun they describe. This means that they have different endings depending on whether the noun is masculine, feminine, singular or plural.

Regular adjectives – e.g. noir

	masculine	*feminine*
singular (s.)	–	add **e**
plural (pl.)	add **s**	add **es**

le chat (m.) noir, les chats (m.pl.) noir**s**
la veste (f.) noir**e**, les vestes (f.pl.) noir**es**

Other adjectives

- Adjectives ending in **e** (masculine singular) do not change in the feminine, e.g. **rouge**, **le sac rouge**, **la chaise rouge**.
- Adjectives ending in **s** or **x** (masculine singular) do not change in the masculine plural, e.g. **j'ai les yeux gris** (*I have grey eyes*).
- Adjectives ending in **eux** (masculine singular) change to **euse** in the feminine, e.g. **un film ennuyeux** (*a boring film*), **une histoire ennuyeuse** (*a boring story*).
- Adjectives ending in **f** (masculine singular) change to **ve** in the feminine, e.g. **un garçon sportif** (*a 'sporty' boy*), **une fille sportive** (*a 'sporty' girl*).
- Some adjectives double the final consonant before adding an **e**, e.g. **un sac violet** (*a purple bag*), **une veste violette** (*a purple jacket*).

Continued overleaf

Beware!

- Some adjectives go in front of the noun. Here are some common ones.

	masc.sing.	*fem.sing.*	*masc.pl.*	*fem.pl.*
beautiful	beau	belle	beaux	belles
good	bon	bonne	bons	bonnes
big/tall	grand	grande	grands	grandes
big/fat	gros	grosse	gros	grosses
attractive	joli	jolie	jolis	jolies
bad	mauvais	mauvaise	mauvais	mauvaises
small	petit	petite	petits	petites
old	vieux	vieille	vieux	vieilles

Age

To say how old you are, use the right part of the verb **avoir** (*to have*). In French you 'have' an age – literally 'I have 14 years'.

J'ai quatorze ans.	*I'm 14 (years old).*
Tu as quinze ans.	*You are 15 (years old).*
Il a treize ans.	*He is 13 (years old).*
Elle a douze ans.	*She is 12 (years old).*
On a douze ans. Nous avons douze ans. }	*We are 12 (years old).*
Vous avez vingt ans.	*You are 20 (years old).*
Ils ont dix ans.	*They are 10 (years old).*
Elles ont onze ans.	*They are 11 (years old).*

Useful questions

Quel âge as-tu?	*How old are you?*
Quelle est la date de ton anniversaire?	*What's the date of your birthday?*
(C'est le 6 mai.)	*(It's the 6th of May.)*

SEE ALSO Birthday

Animals – les animaux

Pets

un animal domestique	*pet*
une araignée	*spider*
un chat	*cat*
un cheval	*horse*
un chien	*dog*
un cochon d'Inde	*guinea pig*
un hamster	*hamster*
un lapin	*rabbit*
un oiseau	*bird*
une perruche	*budgerigar*
un poisson rouge	*goldfish*
une souris	*mouse*
une tortue	*tortoise*

Farm animals

un agneau	*lamb*
un âne	*donkey*
un canard	*duck*
une chèvre	*goat*
un cochon	*pig*
un mouton	*sheep*
une poule	*hen*
une vache	*cow*

Wild animals

une baleine	*whale*
un éléphant	*elephant*
un lion	*lion*
un ours	*bear*
un singe	*monkey*
un tigre	*tiger*

Birthday – l'anniversaire

Quelle est la date de ton anniversaire?   *What is the date of your birthday?*
C'est le 18 janvier.   *It's the 18th of January.*

SEE ALSO Age

Body – le corps

la bouche	*mouth*	le genou	*knee*
le bras	*arm*	la gorge	*throat*
les cheveux	*hair*	la jambe	*leg*
le cœur	*heart*	la main	*hand*
le cou	*neck*	le nez	*nose*
le coude	*elbow*	la tête	*head*
les dents	*teeth*	le visage	*face*
le dos	*back*	les yeux	*eyes*
l'épaule (f.)	*shoulder*		

SEE ALSO Health

Cinema – le cinéma

un dessin animé	*cartoon*	un film policier	*detective film*
un film d'amour	*romance/love film*	un film à suspense	*thriller*
		un western	*western*
un film d'aventures	*adventure film*	une star ⎫	
un film d'espionnage	*spy film*	une vedette ⎭	*film star*
un film d'épouvante ⎫			
un film d'horreur ⎭	*horror film*		

SEE ALSO Television

Classroom – la salle de classe

l'affiche (f.)	poster	dans mon sac	in my bag
la chaise	chair	un agenda	diary
l'écran (m.)	screen	un cahier	exercise book
l'étagère (f.)	shelf	une calculette	calculator
la fenêtre	window	un crayon	pencil
le mur	wall	une gomme	eraser
l'ordinateur (m.)	computer	un livre	book
le placard	cupboard	une règle	ruler
la porte	door	un stylo	pen
la poubelle	bin	un taille-crayon	pencil sharpener
le rétroprojecteur	overhead projector		
la table	table		
le tableau	board		

Clothes – les vêtements

les baskets (m.pl.)	trainers	le jogging	tracksuit
le blouson	jacket	la jupe	skirt
la casquette	baseball cap	le maillot de bain	swimsuit
la ceinture	belt	le manteau	coat
le chapeau	hat	le pantalon	trousers
les chaussettes (f.pl.)	socks	le pullover	jumper
les chaussures (f.pl.)	shoes	la robe	dress
la chemise	shirt	le sac	bag
le chemisier	blouse	le short	shorts
le chouchou	scrunchy	le tee-shirt	T-shirt
le collant	tights		
le complet	suit	**Useful phrases**	
l'écharpe (f.)	scarf	en cuir	in/made of leather
les gants (m.pl.)	gloves	en coton	in/made of cotton
l'imperméable (m.)	raincoat	en laine	in/made of wool
le jean	jeans		

Colours – les couleurs

Colours are adjectives – they agree with the noun they describe.

le chat noir (m.s.)   **les chats noirs (m.pl.)**
la robe bleue (f.s.)   **les robes bleues (f.pl.)**

blanc (m.)		noir	*black*
blanche (f.)	*white*	rose	*pink*
bleu	*blue*	rouge	*red*
brun	*brown*	vert	*green*
gris	*grey*	violet	*purple*
jaune	*yellow*		
marron	*brown*		

(NB this colour does not need to change its endings – it always stays in the same form!)

If you want to say a colour is 'light' or 'dark', you add **clair** or **foncé** after the colour. Note that in these cases, the spelling of the colour adjective doesn't change.

bleu clair	*light blue*
bleu foncé	*dark blue*
vert clair	*light green*
vert foncé	*dark green*

e.g. une robe bleu clair; des robes bleu foncé

Beware! The adjective **orange** also stays the same, however many people or things it is describing.

Compass points

l'est (m.)	*east*
le nord	*north*
l'ouest (m.)	*west*
le sud	*south*

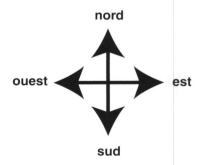

Countries – les pays

l'Allemagne (f.)	*Germany*	la Grèce	*Greece*
l'Angleterre (f.)	*England*	l'Irlande (f.)	*Ireland*
la Belgique	*Belgium*	l'Italie (f.)	*Italy*
le Danemark	*Denmark*	le Luxembourg	*Luxembourg*
l'Écosse (f.)	*Scotland*	le Pays de Galles	*Wales*
l'Espagne (f.)	*Spain*	les Pays-Bas (m.pl.)	*Netherlands*
les États-Unis (m.pl.)	*United States*	le Portugal	*Portugal*
la France	*France*		

'In' or 'to' a country
For **feminine** countries, use **en**
    J'habite en Angleterre, en France, etc.   *I live in England, in France, etc.*
For **masculine** countries, use **au**
    Je vais au Portugal.   *I'm going to Portugal.*
For **plural** countries, use **aux**
    Je vais aux États-Unis.   *I'm going to the United States.*

Feminine countries usually end in an *e*.

EXAM TIP

SEE ALSO Languages, Nationalities

Daily routine

Je me réveille.	*I wake up.*	Je rentre.	*I go home.*
Je me lève.	*I get up.*	Je regarde la	*I watch TV.*
Je me lave.	*I wash.*	télévision.	
Je me brosse les dents.	*I brush my teeth.*	Je prends le dîner.	*I have tea/ evening meal.*
Je m'habille.	*I get dressed.*	Je fais mes devoirs.	*I do my homework.*
Je prends le petit déjeuner.	*I have breakfast.*	Je me repose.	*I relax.*
Je vais au collège.	*I go to school.*	Je me couche.	*I go to bed.*

SEE ALSO Household jobs, Reflexive verbs, Time

Days of the week and parts of the day

lundi	*Monday*	le matin	*the morning*
mardi	*Tuesday*	l'après-midi	*the afternoon*
mercredi	*Wednesday*	le soir	*the evening*
jeudi	*Thursday*	la nuit	*the night*
vendredi	*Friday*	le jour	*the day*
samedi	*Saturday*	tous les jours	*every day*
dimanche	*Sunday*		

Descriptions

Use the verb **avoir** to describe hair and eyes.

J'ai	**les cheveux...**	
Tu as	blonds	*blond hair*
Il a	bruns	*brown hair*
Elle a	gris	*grey hair*
Nous avons	noirs	*black hair*
Vous avez	roux	*ginger/red hair*
Ils ont	bouclés	*curly hair*
Elles ont	courts	*short hair*
	en brosse	*spiky hair*
	longs	*long hair*
	raids	*straight hair*

J'ai (etc.)	**les yeux...**	
	bleus	*blue eyes*
	bruns/marron	*brown eyes*
	gris	*grey eyes*
	noisette	*hazel eyes*
	verts	*green eyes*

Note also:

une barbe	*beard*
une moustache	*moustache*
Je porte des lunettes.	*I wear glasses.*

Use the verb **être** to describe size and character.
Remember to add **s** to the adjective if the subject is plural. (Add **x** to **beau** for plural.)

Je suis	beau/belle	*handsome/beautiful*
Tu es	grand/grande	*tall/big*
Il est	gros/grosse	*fat*
Elle est	joli/jolie	*pretty*
Nous sommes	laid/laide	*ugly*
Vous êtes		
Ils sont	de taille moyenne	*of average height*
Elles sont		

Je suis (etc.)	actif/active	*active*
	agréable	*pleasant*
	aimable	*friendly*
	amusant/amusante	*amusing*
	bête	*stupid*
	calme	*calm*
	content/contente	*pleased/happy*
	dingue	*crazy/mad*
	drôle	*funny*
	fâché/fâchée	*angry*
	heureux/heureuse	*happy*
	honnête	*honest*
	intelligent/intelligente	*clever*
	marrant/marrante	*funny*
	méchant/méchante	*naughty/nasty*
	sage	*well behaved*
	sérieux/sérieuse	*serious*
	sympa	*nice*
	timide	*shy*
	travailleur/travailleuse	*hard working*

SEE ALSO Adjectives

Directions

à droite	*on the right*
à gauche	*on the left*
tout droit	*straight on*
allez tout droit	*go straight on*
prenez la première rue à droite	*take the first road on the right*
prenez la deuxième rue à gauche	*take the second road on the left*
tournez à gauche	*turn left*
traversez le pont	*cross the bridge*
à côté de	*next to*
après	*after*
avant	*before*
devant	*in front of*
derrière	*behind*
en face de	*opposite*

Drinks – les boissons

Je voudrais	*I'd like*		
une bière	*beer*	de l'eau minérale	*mineral water*
un café	*black coffee*	un jus d'orange	*orange juice*
un café-crème	*white coffee*	un jus de pomme	*apple juice*
un chocolat chaud	*hot chocolate*	un orangina	*Orangina™*
un citron pressé	*fresh lemon juice*	un thé (au lait)	*tea (with milk)*
		(un) vin blanc	*white wine*
un coca	*Coca Cola™*	(un) vin rouge	*red wine*

SEE ALSO Eating out, Food

Eating out

Places to eat

le bistro	*bistro*
le café	*café*
la pizzeria	*pizzeria*
le restaurant	*restaurant*
le restaurant rapide	*fast-food restaurant*

People

le caissier/la caissière	*check-out/till operator*
le chef	*chef*
le client/la cliente	*customer*
le garçon	*waiter*
le patron/la patronne	*owner*
la serveuse	*waitress*

General

l'addition (f.)	*bill*
les boissons (f.pl.)	*drinks*
la carte	*menu*
le dessert	*dessert*
l'entrée (f.)	*starter*
le menu	*fixed-price menu*
le plat du jour	*dish of the day*
le plat principal	*main course*
le pourboire	*tip*
service compris	*service included*
la terrasse	*terrace*

Useful phrases

Je voudrais…	*I'd like…*
Avez-vous…?	*Do you have…?*
L'addition, s'il vous plaît.	*The bill, please.*
Le service est compris?	*Is the service charge included?*
Où sont les toilettes?	*Where are the toilets?*
Je n'ai pas de (verre).	*I haven't got a (glass).*

SEE ALSO Drinks, Food, Meals

Family – la famille

le beau-père	*stepfather*	la grand-mère	*grandmother*
la belle-mère	*stepmother*	les grands-parents (m.pl.)	*grandparents*
le cousin/la cousine	*cousin*		
le demi-frère	*half brother*	le grand-père	*grandfather*
la demi-sœur	*half sister*	maman	*Mum*
l'enfant (m./f.)	*child*	le mari	*husband*
la famille	*family*	la mère	*mother*
la femme	*woman/wife*	papa	*Dad*
le/la fiancé(e)	*fiancé(e)*	les parents (m.pl.)	*parents*
la fille	*girl/daughter*	le père	*father*
le fils	*son*	les petits-enfants (m.pl.)	*grandchildren*
le frère	*brother*		
le garçon	*boy*		

Festivals – les fêtes

le jour de l'An	*New Year's Day*	**Useful verbs and phrases**	
le jour de Noël	*Christmas Day*	acheter	*to buy*
le jour de Pâques	*Easter Day*	envoyer	*to send*
le jour des Rois	*Twelfth Night/ Epiphany*	fêter	*to celebrate*
		offrir un cadeau	*to give a present*
le Ramadan	*Ramadan*	C'est quand, ton anniversaire?	*When is your birthday?*
le Réveillon (du Nouvel An)	*New Year's Eve*		
		On écrit des cartes.	*People write cards.*
le Sabbat	*Sabbath*		
la Veille de Noël	*Christmas Eve*	On décore des œufs.	*People decorate eggs.*
l'anniversaire (m.)	*birthday*		
l'arbre de Noël (m.)	*Christmas tree*	On offre des cadeaux.	*People give presents.*
le cadeau	*present*		
la carte	*card*	On invite la famille/ les amis.	*People invite the family/friends.*
le gâteau	*cake*		
le repas de Noël	*Christmas dinner*	On va à l'église.	*People go to church.*
le père Noël	*Father Christmas*		
		On mange beaucoup.	*People eat a lot.*

Food – l'alimentation

General

la baguette	*French stick*
le beurre	*butter*
les bonbons (m.pl.)	*sweets*
les chips (m.pl.)	*crisps*
le chocolat	*chocolate*
la confiture	*jam*
le croissant	*croissant*
le fromage	*cheese*
le gâteau	*cake*
la glace	*ice cream*
l'huile (f.)	*oil*
le lait	*milk*
les œufs (m.pl.)	*eggs*
le pain	*bread*
les pâtes (f.pl.)	*pasta*
la pizza	*pizza*
le riz	*rice*
le sucre	*sugar*
le yaourt	*yoghurt*

Meat – la viande

l'agneau (m.)	*lamb*
le bifteck	*steak*
le bœuf	*beef*
le canard	*duck*
la dinde	*turkey*
le jambon	*ham*
le lapin	*rabbit*
le mouton	*mutton*
le porc	*pork*
le poulet	*chicken*
le rôti	*roast meat*
le saucisson	*cured pork sausage*
le steak	*steak*

Fish – le poisson

les crevettes (f.pl.)	*prawns*
les fruits de mer (m.pl.)	*shellfish/ seafood*
les moules (f.pl.)	*mussels*
le poisson	*fish*

Fruit – les fruits

l'abricot (m.)	*apricot*
la banane	*banana*
la cerise	*cherry*
le citron	*lemon*
la fraise	*strawberry*
la framboise	*raspberry*
le melon	*melon*
l'orange (f.)	*orange*
le pamplemousse	*grapefruit*
la pêche	*peach*
la poire	*pear*
la pomme	*apple*
la prune	*plum*
le raisin	*grape*

Vegetables – les légumes

l'ail (m.)	*garlic*
la carotte	*carrot*
le champignon	*mushroom*
le chou	*cabbage*
le chou-fleur	*cauliflower*
l'haricot (m.)	*bean*
l'haricot vert (m.)	*green/French bean*
l'oignon (m.)	*onion*
les petits pois (m.pl.)	*peas*
les pommes de terre (f.pl.)	*potatoes*
la tomate	*tomato*

SEE ALSO Drinks, Eating out, Meals

Free time – going out

la boîte	*disco*	le jardin public	*park*
la boum	*party*	les magasins (m.pl.)	*shops*
le centre sportif	*sports centre*	la patinoire	*ice rink*
le cinéma	*cinema*	la piscine	*swimming pool*
le club des jeunes	*youth club*	le stade	*stadium*
la discothèque	*disco*	le théâtre	*theatre*

Useful phrases

Tu veux aller au cinéma?	*Do you want to go to the cinema?*
Tu veux aller à la patinoire?	*Do you want to go to the ice rink?*
Si on sortait ce soir?	*How about going out this evening?*
Je voudrais aller au cinéma.	*I'd like to go to the cinema.*
Je veux bien!	*I'd love to!*
Je ne peux pas!	*I can't!*
Où veux-tu aller?	*Where do you want to go?*

Last weekend

Le weekend dernier, je suis allé(e) au cinéma avec mes amis.
 J'ai vu un bon film.
Last weekend, I went to the cinema with my friends. I saw a good film.

Arranging to meet

On se rencontre à quelle heure?	*What time shall we meet?*
Où est-ce qu'on se rencontre?	*Where shall we meet?*

EXAM TIP

If you go to a place, remember:
  à + le = au   Je vais au cinéma.
  à + la = à la   Je vais à la piscine.
  à + les = aux   Je vais aux magasins.

Free time – at home

Useful verbs and phrases

aimer   *to like*

Use **j'aime** in front of the expressions below to say what you like doing.

aller en ville	*to go to town*	je vais en ville
bricoler	*to do DIY*	je bricole
chanter	*to sing*	je chante
collectionner	*to collect*	je collectionne
danser	*to dance*	je danse
dessiner	*to draw*	je dessine
écouter	*to listen to*	j'écoute
faire les magasins	*to go round the shops/to 'do' the shops*	je fais les magasins
jouer (aux cartes)	*to play (cards)*	je joue
lire	*to read*	je lis
regarder	*to watch*	je regarde
se promener*	*to go for a walk*	je me promène
surfer sur Internet/le net	*to surf the net*	je surfe sur Internet

* after **j'aime**, use **me promener**, not **se promener**.

Le soir – in the evening

J'écoute des CD/la radio.	*I listen to CDs/the radio.*
Je fais un jeu d'ordinateur.	*I play a computer game.*
Je joue de la musique.	*I play music.*
Je joue de la batterie.	*I play the drums.*
Je lis.	*I read.*
Je regarde la télé.	*I watch TV.*

SEE ALSO Holidays, Sports, Television

Future tense (near future)

The near future is the same as 'going to do' in English.

Je vais acheter un livre.   *I am going to buy a book.*

Je vais regarder la télévision.   *I am going to watch TV.*

It is very simple to use the near future. You need two things:

1   present tense of **aller** (e.g. **je vais**)

    plus

2   the infinitive (name of the verb) (e.g. **regarder**).

    Je *vais regarder* la télévision.

EXAM TIP

aller = je vais, tu vas, il/elle/on va, nous allons, vous allez, ils/elles vont

Gender

In French, all nouns (naming words) are either masculine or feminine (gender). You need to learn whether a noun is masculine or feminine when you learn the word.

the = *le/la/les*

le = masculine (**le sac**) **la** = feminine (**la table**)

- Both **le** and **la** mean 'the' in English.
- If a noun starts with a vowel, use **l'** (**l'église**).
- A plural noun has **les** in front of it whether the noun is masculine or feminine.

    les sacs (m.pl.)   **les tables** (f.pl.)   **les églises** (f.pl.)

a/some = *un/une/des*

    un sac (m.) = *a bag*   **une table** (f.) = *a table*
    des sacs = *some bags*   **des tables** = *some tables*

SEE ALSO Nouns

Greetings

Bonjour, Monsieur/ Madame.	*Good morning/ afternoon.*	Ça va?	*How are you?*
Bonsoir, Monsieur/ Madame.	*Good evening.*	Ça va bien, merci.	*Very well, thank you.*
Salut!	*Hi!*	Je te présente Claire.	*May I introduce you to Claire?*
Au revoir.	*Goodbye.*		
À bientôt.	*See you soon.*	Enchanté(e).	*Delighted to meet you.*
À tout à l'heure.	*See you later.*	Merci.	*Thank you.*
À demain.	*See you tomorrow.*	Pardon/Excusez-moi.	*Excuse me.*
		S'il vous plaît.	*Please.*

Health – la santé

Useful vocabulary and phrases

avoir mal à	*to have a pain*

Use this with a part of the body to say where you have a pain.

J'ai mal au genou.	*My knee hurts.*
J'ai mal à la gorge.	*My throat hurts.*
J'ai mal aux yeux.	*My eyes hurt.*
Je suis allergique à…	*I'm allergic to…*
Je suis enrhumé(e).	*I've got a cold.*
Je suis malade.	*I'm ill.*
Je suis en forme.	*I'm fine/on form.*
Je me suis cassé la jambe.	*I've broken my leg.*
J'ai froid.	*I'm cold.*
J'ai chaud.	*I'm hot.*
J'ai de la fièvre.	*I've got a temperature.*
Je suis fatigué(e).	*I'm tired.*
J'ai soif.	*I'm thirsty.*

At the chemist's – à la pharmacie

une aspirine	*aspirin*
des comprimés (m.pl.)	*tablets*
la crème anti-solaire	*sun protection cream*
la cuillerée	*spoonful*
le dentifrice	*toothpaste*
le pansement	*dressing*
la pastille	*lozenge*
le/la pharmacien(ne)	*chemist*
la piqûre (d'insecte)	*(insect) bite*
le sirop	*medicine (syrup)*
le sparadrap	*plaster*

General

une ordonnance	*prescription*
un rendez-vous	*appointment*

SEE ALSO Body

Holidays – les vacances

General

la carte	map	le séjour	stay
le dépliant	brochure	les vacances (f.pl.)	holidays
l'office de tourisme	tourist information office	la valise	case
		la visite	visit
le passeport	passport	le voyage	journey
le plan (de la ville)	(town) plan		

Camping

le bloc sanitaire	toilet block	le feu	fire
le bureau d'accueil	reception	la piscine	pool
le campeur	camper	le sac de couchage	sleeping bag
le camping	camping	la salle de jeux	games room
la caravane	caravan	la tente	tent
l'eau potable (f.)	drinking water	à l'ombre	in the shade
l'eau non-potable (f.)	non-drinking water	au soleil	in the sun
l'électricité (f.)	electricity		
l'emplacement (m.)	pitch		

Hotel

l'ascenseur (m.)	lift	le parking	car park
le bain	bath	le patron	owner
le balcon	balcony	la pension complète	full board
la chambre	bedroom	le petit déjeuner	breakfast
cher, chère	expensive	la réception	reception
la clé	key	le restaurant	restaurant
la demi-pension	half board	le rez-de-chaussée	ground floor
la douche	shower	la salle de bains	bathroom
l'escalier (m.)	staircase	la sortie de secours	emergency exit
l'étage (m.)	floor (e.g. 2nd floor)	les toilettes (f.pl.)	toilets
l'hôtel (m.)	hotel		

Youth hostel

l'auberge de jeunesse (f.)	youth hostel
le bureau	office
la carte d'adhérent	membership card
complet, complète	full
la couverture	blanket
la cuisine	kitchen
le dortoir	dormitory

l'eau chaude (f.)	hot water
fermé	closed
le linge	linen
ouvert	open
la poubelle	bin
le sac à dos	rucksack
la salle à manger	dining room
le silence	silence

Places to go

Je vais à la campagne.	I go to the countryside.
Je vais à la montagne.	I go to the mountains.
Je vais au bord de la mer.	I go to the seaside.

Places to stay

Je fais du camping.	I go camping.
Je reste à l'hôtel.	I stay at the hotel.
Je reste à l'auberge de jeunesse.	I stay at the youth hostel.
Je reste chez des amis.	I stay with friends.

Useful phrases

Je voudrais une/deux chambre(s)	I'd like one/two rooms
… pour deux personnes	… for two people
… avec un grand lit	… with a double bed
… avec deux lits	… with twin beds
… avec salle de bains	… with a bathroom
… avec douche	… with a shower
… pour deux nuits	… for two nights
… pour une semaine	… for a week

Continued overleaf

Où est	Where is
... le jardin?	... the garden?
... le parking?	... the car park?
... la piscine?	... the pool?
... le dortoir?	... the dormitory?
... la salle à manger?	... the dining room?

Je voudrais réserver un emplacement pour une tente.
I'd like to reserve a pitch for a tent.
Avez-vous des places pour ce soir?
Have you any places for tonight? (youth hostel)
Avez-vous des chambres?
Have you any rooms? (hotel)

Be prepared to say what you do on holiday.

Je nage.	*I swim.*	Je vais en boîte.	*I go to clubs/ discos.*
Je joue au tennis.	*I play tennis.*		
Je joue au volley.	*I play volleyball.*	Je vais au restaurant.	*I go to restaurants.*
Je fais de la planche à voile.	*I go windsurfing.*	Je me bronze.	*I sunbathe.*
Je vais à la plage.	*I go to the beach.*	Je me promène.	*I go for walks.*

If you want to talk about last year's holiday, use the following expressions:

L'anneé dernière...	*Last year...*
je suis allé(e) en France.	*I went to France...*
j'ai visité...	*I visited...*
j'ai vu...	*I saw...*
j'ai joué...	*I played...*

SEE ALSO Free time – going out, Past (perfect) tense

Home/house – chez moi/la maison

Places to live

un appartement	*flat*
une ferme	*farm*
une HLM	*council flat*
un immeuble	*block of flats*
une maison	*house*
un pavillon	*detached house*

Rooms/places in the home

la buanderie	*utility room*
le bureau	*office*
la cave	*cellar*
la chambre (à coucher)	*bedroom*
la cuisine	*kitchen*
l'entrée (f.)	*hall*
en bas	*downstairs*
en haut	*upstairs*
le garage	*garage*
le grenier	*attic*
le jardin	*garden*
la salle à manger	*dining room*
la salle de bains	*bathroom*
la salle de séjour⎫ le salon ⎭	*living room/ lounge*
le sous-sol	*basement*
la terrasse	*terrace*
le vestibule	*hall*
les w.c. (m.pl.)	*toilet*

Continued overleaf

Furniture/fittings

l'armoire (f.)	wardrobe
la chaise	chair
la coiffeuse	dressing table
la lampe	lamp
le lit	bed
la moquette	fitted carpet
les rideaux (m.pl.)	curtains
la cuisine	kitchen
la cuisinière	cooker
le congélateur	freezer
l'évier (m.)	sink
le four à micro-ondes	microwave
le frigo	fridge
le lave-vaisselle	dishwasher
le lave-linge/la machine à laver	washing machine
le placard	cupboard
la douche	shower
le lavabo	washbasin
l'étagère (f.)	shelf
le canapé	sofa
la chaîne hi-fi	music centre
le fauteuil	armchair
le lecteur de CD	CD player
le lecteur de DVD	DVD player
le magnétoscope	video
la télévision	television

Home life

Dans ma chambre...	*In my room...*
Je fais mes devoirs.	I do my homework.
Je joue avec mon ordinateur.	I play with my computer.
J'écoute de la musique.	I listen to music.
J'écoute mes CD.	I listen to my CDs.
Je regarde la télévision.	I watch TV.
Je lis.	I read.
Je dors.	I sleep.

Dans la cuisine…
Je prends le petit déjeuner.
Je prépare les repas.
Je mange.

In the kitchen…
I eat breakfast.
I prepare meals.
I eat.

Dans le salon…
Je regarde la télévision.
J'écoute de la musique.
Je parle avec mes amis.
Je me repose.

In the living room…
I watch TV.
I listen to music.
I talk with my friends.
I relax.

SEE ALSO Daily routine, Household jobs

Household jobs

Useful phrases using the verb *faire*

Je fais du bricolage.
Je fais la cuisine.
Je fais les courses.
Je fais du jardinage.
Je fais le ménage.
Je fais la vaisselle.
Je fais mon lit.

I do odd jobs/DIY.
I do the cooking.
I do the shopping.
I do the gardening.
I do the housework.
I do the washing up.
I make my bed.

Other useful expressions

Je mets la table.
Je débarrasse la table.
Je sors la poubelle.

I set the table.
I clear the table.
I take the rubbish out.

SEE ALSO Daily routine

Imperfect tense

At this stage, you do not need to know how the whole of this tense works, but a
few expressions will help you to describe things in the past.

C'était   *It was*
Il y avait   *There was, there were*
J'étais   *I was*
e.g. J'étais content(e).   *I was happy.*

(This one is useful for describing how you felt in the past.)

Il faisait is useful for describing weather in the past.

Il faisait chaud.   *It was hot.*

Jobs – le travail

Je voudrais travailler.   *I'd like to work.*
Il/Elle travaille.   *He/She works.*

Places

dans un bureau	*in an office*
dans une école	*in a school*
dans un magasin	*in a shop*
dans une usine	*in a factory*
à la gare	*at the station*
à la maison	*at home*
en plein air	*outside/in the open air*

Jobs

un agent de police	*police officer*
un chauffeur d'autobus	*bus driver*
un coiffeur/une coiffeuse	*hairdresser*
un électricien	*electrician*
un(e) employé(e) des PTT	*post-office worker*
un facteur	*postman*
un fermier	*farmer*
un fonctionnaire	*civil servant*
un infirmier/une infirmière	*nurse*
un informaticien/une informaticienne	*computer scientist*
un ingénieur	*engineer*
un instituteur/une institutrice	*primary teacher*
un maçon	*builder*
un mécanicien	*mechanic*
un médecin	*doctor*
un pompier	*firefighter*
un professeur	*teacher (secondary)*
un(e) secrétaire	*secretary*
un technicien/une technicienne	*technician*
un vendeur/une vendeuse	*sales assistant*

EXAM TIP

To say what somebody does, miss out the *un/une*.
Il est pompier.   *He is a firefighter.*
Elle est médecin.   *She is a doctor.*

Languages – les langues

allemand	*German*	gallois	*Welsh*
anglais	*English*	grec	*Greek*
espagnol	*Spanish*	irlandais	*Irish*
français	*French*	italien	*Italian*

Languages in French start with a small letter, not a capital.
En France, on parle français!   *In France, people speak French!*

SEE ALSO Countries, Nationalities

Meals – les repas

le petit déjeuner	*breakfast*
le déjeuner	*lunch/midday meal*
le dîner ⎫ le repas du soir ⎭	*dinner, evening meal*
le goûter	*afternoon snack*
le pique-nique	*picnic*

SEE ALSO Eating out, Food

Money – l'argent

l'argent (m.)	*money*	la livre	*pound (sterling)*
l'argent de poche	*pocket money*	la monnaie	*change*
le billet	*banknote*	la pièce	*coin*
l'euro (m.)	*Euro*		

Useful questions

C'est combien?	*How much is it?*
Ça coûte combien?	*How much does it cost?*

Months – les mois

janvier	*January*	juillet	*July*
février	*February*	août	*August*
mars	*March*	septembre	*September*
avril	*April*	octobre	*October*
mai	*May*	novembre	*November*
juin	*June*	décembre	*December*

Remember:
* The months do not start with a capital letter in French.
* To say 'in' a month, use **en**, e.g. **en janvier**.

Nationalities

All these nationalities are adjectives so they have masculine and feminine versions (usually add an **e** for a feminine version).

Je suis...	*I am...*	gallois(e)	*Welsh*
allemand(e)	*German*	grec/grecque	*Greek*
anglais(e)	*English*	indien/indienne	*Indian*
belge	*Belgian*	irlandais(e)	*Irish*
écossais(e)	*Scottish*	italien/italienne	*Italian*
espagnol(e)	*Spanish*	japonais(e)	*Japanese*
français(e)	*French*		

Useful phrases

Où es-tu né(e)?	*Where were you born?*
Je suis né(e) à Bath.	*I was born in Bath.*
De quelle nationalité es-tu?	*What nationality are you?*

SEE ALSO Countries, Languages

Negatives

If a negative is used in a sentence, it is like saying 'not' in English.

Je mange.	*I eat.*
Je ne mange pas.	*I do not eat.*

To make a negative statement in French, put **ne** in front of the verb and **pas** after it.

Je regarde la télévision.	*I watch TV.*
Je **ne** regarde **pas** la télévision.	*I do not watch TV.*
Il aime le chocolat.	*He likes chocolate.*
Il **n'**aime **pas** le chocolat.	*He doesn't like chocolate.*

Before a vowel the **ne** becomes **n'**. If you want to use a negative before **un**, **une**, **du**, **de la**, **de l'** or **des** ('a', 'any' or 'some'), you need to use the word **de** instead.

Je **n'**ai pas **de** frères.	*I haven't got any brothers.*
Je **n'**ai pas **de** bonbons.	*I haven't got any sweets.*

There are other useful negatives:

ne … jamais	*never*
Je **ne** mange **jamais** de fromage.	*I never eat cheese.*
ne … plus	*no longer/more*
Je **n'**ai **plus** d'argent.	*I have no more money.*
ne … rien	*nothing*
Il **ne** mange **rien**.	*He eats nothing (doesn't eat anything).*

In the perfect tense, the negative wraps around the auxiliary verb **avoir** or **être**.

Je **n'ai pas** mangé.	*I haven't eaten.*
Je **ne suis pas** parti(e).	*I didn't leave.*
Elle **n'est pas** allée en ville.	*She didn't go to town.*

SEE ALSO Verbs

Nouns

Nouns are naming words for people or things. In French, all nouns have a gender (masculine or feminine). Learn the gender when you learn the noun.

le sac (m.)	*the bag*
la trousse (f.)	*the pencil case*

SEE ALSO Gender

Numbers

1	un, une	18	dix-huit	70	soixante-dix
2	deux	19	dix-neuf	71	soixante et onze
3	trois	20	vingt	72	soixante-douze
4	quatre	21	vingt et un	73	soixante-treize
5	cinq	22	vingt-deux	80	quatre-vingts
6	six	23	vingt-trois	81	quatre-vingt-un
7	sept	24	vingt-quatre	82	quatre-vingt-deux
8	huit	25	vingt-cinq	83	quatre-vingt-trois
9	neuf	26	vingt-six	90	quatre-vingt-dix
10	dix	27	vingt-sept	91	quatre-vingt-onze
11	onze	28	vingt-huit	92	quatre-vingt-douze
12	douze	29	vingt-neuf		
13	treize	30	trente		
14	quatorze	31	trente et un		
15	quinze	40	quarante		
16	seize	50	cinquante		
17	dix-sept	60	soixante		

100	cent
101	cent un
150	cent cinquante
200	deux cents
1000	mille
1 000 000	un million

To give a date

le 12 mai	le douze mai	*the twelfth (12th) of May*
le 20 juillet	le vingt juillet	*the twentieth (20th) of July*

However, the first of the month is **le premier** not **le un**!

le premier janvier   *the first (1st) of January*

For other numbers which have an order, e.g. first, second, third, etc., use the following:

premier/première	*first*
deuxième	*second*
troisième	*third*
quatrième	*fourth*

Opinions

Remember, the verb **aimer** (*to like*) and the negative version are useful to give opinions.

Je n'aime pas   *I don't like*

- Here are some other useful positive opinions:

+

C'est…
bien	*good*
chouette	*great*
cool	*cool*
fantastique	*fantastic*
génial	*great*
intéressant	*interesting*
super	*super/great*

- Here are some negative opinions:

–

C'est…
affreux	*awful (horrible)*
bête	*stupid*
barbant } ennuyeux }	*boring*
moche	*awful (ugly, nasty)*
nul	*terrible (worth nothing)*

If you want to give an opinion about something in the past, use **c'était** instead of **c'est**.

C'était intéressant.   *It was interesting.*

Partitive article (some/any)

There are five different ways to say *some/any*: **du**, **de la**, **de l'**, **des**, **de**.
You need to choose the article to match the noun.

masculine singular
le vin	*the wine*
du vin	*some wine*

feminine singular
la viande	*the meat*
de la viande	*some meat*

nouns (m. or f.) starting with a vowel or silent h
l'eau	*the water*
de l'eau	*some water*
l'huile	*the oil*
de l'huile	*some oil*

Continued overleaf

plural nouns (m. or f.)

les bananes	*the bananas*
des bananes	*some bananas*

But remember, after a negative use **de** instead of the above.

Je n'ai pas de vin.	*I haven't any wine.*
Je n'ai pas de pommes.	*I haven't any apples.*
Je n'ai pas d'argent.	*I haven't any money.*

Past (perfect) tense

The main kind of past tense which you need to know at this stage is the perfect tense. This tense tells us what happened in the past. It is often described as the tense of *finished* actions – something which happened once in the past, e.g. 'I got up', 'I had breakfast', 'I went to school'. Each of these verbs describes a finished action – a bit like a series of events in a story which took place last year, last week or even five minutes ago.

How to make the perfect tense
You need two parts to make this tense:

1 An auxiliary verb
(always part of the verb **avoir** or **être**, e.g. **j'ai** or **je suis**)

avoir	être
j'ai	je suis
tu as	tu es
il/elle a	il/elle est
nous avons	nous sommes
vous avez	vous êtes
ils/elles ont	ils/elles sont

Certain actions need to use part of the verb **avoir**; certain actions need to use part of the verb **être** (see p.31). Most actions take **avoir**.

2 The past participle
The second thing you need is called the past participle (the past bit of the verb), e.g. 'eaten', 'drunk', 'seen'.

Remember, in French all infinitives end in **er**, **ir** or **re**. Here is how to find the past participle.

er	Take off **er**, add **é**	e.g. regard**er** = regard**é**
ir	Take off **ir**, add **i**	e.g. fin**ir** = fin**i**
re	Take off **re**, add **u**	e.g. vend**re** = vend**u**

Now add the two together.

J'ai mangé.	*I ate/have eaten.*
Tu as fini.	*You finished/have finished.*
J'ai vendu le vélo.	*I sold/have sold the bike.*

The perfect tense with *avoir*

Here is a full verb in the perfect tense:

regarder	***to watch***
j'ai regardé	*I watched*
tu as regardé	*you watched*
il/elle a regardé	*he/she watched*
nous avons regardé	*we watched*
vous avez regardé	*you watched*
ils/elles ont regardé	*they watched*

Here are some **avoir** verbs with irregular past participles:

boire	j'ai bu	*I drank*	lire	j'ai lu	*I read*
dire	j'ai dit	*I said*	mettre	j'ai mis	*I put*
écrire	j'ai écrit	*I wrote*	ouvrir	j'ai ouvert	*I opened*
être	j'ai été	*I have been*	prendre	j'ai pris	*I took/had*
faire	j'ai fait	*I did*	voir	j'ai vu	*I saw*

The perfect tense with *être*

Most verbs take **avoir** as their auxiliary, but some take **être** (**je suis**, etc.).
There is an easy way to remember which ones! Look at the first letter of each.

		Infinitive	*Past participle*
M		**m**onter (*to go up*)	monté
R		**r**ester (*to stay*)	resté
V		**v**enir (*to come*)	venu
A		**a**ller (*to go*)	allé
N		**n**aître (*to be born*)	né
S		**s**ortir (*to go out*)	sorti
T		**t**omber (*to fall*)	tombé
R		**r**etourner (*to return*)	retourné
A		**a**rriver (*to arrive*)	arrivé
M		**m**ourir (*to die*)	mort
P		**p**artir (*to leave*)	parti
E		**e**ntrer (*to go into*)	entré
D		**d**escendre (*to do down*)	descendu

Think! If you need a MR VANS TRAMPED verb in the perfect, use **être**.

Je **suis** allé(e)	*I went*	Je **suis** arrivé(e)	*I arrived*

Continued overleaf

Agreements

If you use a MR VANS TRAMPED verb (one which uses **être** as its auxiliary verb), you need to make the past participle agree with the person (subject).

Je suis parti	*I left (one boy)*
Je suis parti**e**	*I left (one girl)*
Ils sont parti**s**	*They left (more than one boy/boys and girls)*
Elles sont parti**es**	*They left (more than one girl)*

It's just like adjectives – add **e** for feminine singular, **s** for masculine plural and **es** for feminine plural.

Je suis allé**e** en ville.   *I went to town. (one female)*

EXAM TIP

Look for time markers to show when to use the perfect tense, such as:

l'année dernière	*last year*
la semaine dernière	*last week*
hier	*yesterday*

SEE ALSO Verbs

Permission

Use *je peux* to ask if you can do something.

Je peux ouvrir la fenêtre, s'il vous plaît?
Please can I open the window?
Je peux regarder la télévision, s'il vous plaît?
Can I watch TV, please?

Pets see Animals

Places see Town

Plurals

To make most nouns plural, add an **s** and use **les** (*the*) or **des** (*some*) in front of the noun.

    la pomme *the apple*   **les** pomme**s**   *the apples*

But note:

* Nouns ending in **al** become **aux**.
  un chev**al**   des chev**aux**
* Nouns ending in **au**, **eau** or **eu** add **x**.
  un chât**eau**   des chât**eaux**
* Nouns ending in **s**, **x** or **z** stay the same.
  une souri**s**   des souri**s**

SEE ALSO Nouns

Post office see Shopping

Present tense

The name of a verb (e.g. 'to run' or 'to swim' in English) is called the infinitive. In French, infinitives end in **er**, **ir** or **re**.

The present tense in French describes what is happening now or what usually happens. To make the present tense, check whether the verb you want to use has an infinitive ending in **er**, **ir** or **re**.

For **er** verbs, e.g. **regarder**, take off the **er** and add the endings **e**, **es**, **e**, **ons**, **ez**, **ent**.

je joue	nous jouons
tu joues	vous jouez
il/elle joue	ils/elles jouent

For **ir** verbs, e.g. **finir**, take off the **ir** and add the endings **is**, **is**, **it**, **issons**, **issez**, **issent**.

je finis	nous finissons
tu finis	vous finissez
il/elle finit	ils/elles finissent

Continued overleaf

For **re** verbs, e.g. **vendre**, take off the **re** and add **s**, **s**, nothing, **ons**, **ez**, **ent**.

je vends	nous vendons
tu vends	vous vendez
il/elle vend	ils/elles vendent

Some exceptions to know

j'ai (**avoir**)	*I have*
je fais (**faire**)	*I do*
je suis (**être**)	*I am*
je vais (**aller**)	*I go*

SEE ALSO Verbs

Pronouns

Subject pronouns

Subject pronouns are words like *I*, *you*, *he*, *she*, *we*, *you*, *they*, which are connected to verbs.

> **je** mange   *I eat*

A subject pronoun goes with a verb and tells you who is performing the action.

je	*I*	on	*one/we/people*
tu	*you*	nous	*we*
il	*he*	vous	*you*
elle	*she*	ils/elles	*they*

Subject pronouns go in front of the verb.

je regarde	*I watch*
tu regardes	*you watch*
il/elle regarde	*he/she watches*
nous regardons	*we watch*
vous regardez	*you watch*
ils/elles regardent	*they watch*

Direct object pronouns

Direct object pronouns are words which refer to the person or thing which has an action done to it, such as *it* or *me*.

Il mange la pomme.	*He eats the apple.*
Il **la** mange.	*He eats **it**.*

(*He* is the subject, *the apple* or *it* is the object.)

In French, these words are:

me *(me)*	**nous** *(us)*
te *(you)*	**vous** *(you)*
le/la *(he/she/it)*	**les** *(them)*

They go **before** the verb.

Il **te** regarde.	*He watches **you**.*
Il **les** mange.	*He eats **them**.*

Quantity

Some useful expressions

assez de	*enough*
beaucoup de	*a lot of*
trop de	*too much/too many*

Il y a assez de pain.	*There is enough bread.*
Il y a beaucoup de frites.	*There are a lot of chips.*
Tu manges trop de bonbons!	*You eat too many sweets!*

SEE ALSO Shopping

Questions

There are three ways of asking a question in French.
1 Add a question mark and raise your voice at the end of the sentence.
Tu aimes la glace?   *Do you like ice cream?*

2 Add **est-ce que**.
Est-ce que tu aimes la glace?   *Do you like ice cream?*

3 Turn the subject and verb the other way round, and add a hyphen (-).
Aimes-tu la glace?   *Do you like ice cream?*

Useful question words

À quelle heure?	*At what time?*	Quand...?	*When...?*
Comment...?	*How...?*	Qu'est-ce que...?	*What...?*
Où...?	*Where...?*	Quel/Quelle...?	*Which...?*
Pourquoi...?	*Why...?*	Quels/Quelles...?	

Reflexive verbs

A reflexive verb is used to show an action done to yourself. Look at the difference.

Je me lave.   *I wash (myself).* – reflexive verb
Je lave la voiture.   *I wash the car.* – not a reflexive verb

The **me** is called a reflexive pronoun.
* Reflexive verbs need reflexive pronouns.
* Reflexive verbs can easily be spotted in a dictionary. They have **se** in front of the infinitive.

Here is a reflexive verb, **se laver**:

je me lave   *I get washed/wash (myself)*
tu te laves   *(etc.)*
il/elle se lave
nous nous lavons
vous vous lavez
ils/elles se lavent

Beware! In the perfect tense, reflexive verbs take **être**.

Je me suis levé(e).   *I got up.*
Je me suis lavé(e).   *I got washed.*

Notice also that the ending of the past participle (e.g. **levé(e)**) agrees with the subject (person performing the action).

SEE ALSO Daily routine, Verbs

School – l'école

le collège	secondary school
le CES	
l'école (f.)	school
l'école primaire	primary school
l'élève (m./f.)	pupil
le lycée	sixth-form college
la récréation	break
la rentrée	start of school year
le trimestre	term
les vacances (f.pl.)	holidays

School subjects – les matières scolaires

l'allemand (m.)	German
l'anglais (m.)	English
l'art dramatique (m.)	drama
la biologie	biology
la chimie	chemistry
le dessin	art
l'éducation civique	citizenship/PSHE
l'éducation physique	PE
EPS	
l'éducation religieuse	RE
l'espagnol (m.)	Spanish
le français	French
la géographie	geography
l'histoire (f.)	history
l'informatique (f.)	IT
les maths (m.pl.)	maths
les mathématiques	
la musique	music
la physique	physics
les sciences (f.pl.)	science
la technologie	technology

Continued overleaf

School buildings – les bâtiments scolaires

l'atelier (m.)	*workshop, studio*
la bibliothèque	*library*
la cantine	*canteen*
la cour	*playground*
le laboratoire	*laboratory*
la salle de classe	*classroom*
la salle des professeurs	*staffroom*
les vestiaires (m.pl.)	*changing rooms*

Useful phrases

j'étudie (+ *subject*)	*I study*
j'aime	*I like*
je préfère	*I prefer*
je n'aime pas	*I don't like*
je déteste	*I hate*
C'est amusant.	*It's funny.*
C'est difficile.	*It's difficult.*
C'est facile.	*It's easy.*
C'est intéressant.	*It's interesting.*

Les cours commencent à neuf heures.	*Lessons begin at nine o'clock.*
Les cours finissent à quatre heures.	*Lessons finish at four o'clock.*
Je mange à la cantine.	*I eat in the canteen.*
Je viens au collège en car.	*I come to school by bus.*

Seasons – les saisons

le printemps	*spring*
l'été (m.)	*summer*
l'automne (m.)	*autumn*
l'hiver (m.)	*winter*

For summer, autumn or winter use **en**, e.g. **en hiver** (in winter).
For spring use **au** – **au printemps** (in spring).

Shopping – les courses

l'alimentation générale (f.)	general food shop
l'ascenseur (m.)	lift
la boucherie	butcher's
la boulangerie	baker's
la boutique	small shop
la caisse	checkout
la charcuterie	delicatessen
le coiffeur	hairdresser's
la confiserie	sweet shop
la crémerie	dairy produce shop
l'épicerie (f.)	grocer's
le grand magasin	department store
l'hypermarché (m.)	hypermarket
la librairie	bookshop
les magasins (m.pl.)	shops
le marché	market
la pâtisserie	cake shop
la pharmacie	chemist's
la poissonnerie	fish shop
le prix	price
la quincaillerie	hardware shop
le rayon	department in large shop
la sortie	exit
le supermarché	supermarket
le tabac	tobacconist's

Useful phrases

Je voudrais…	I'd like…
Ça fait combien?	How much is it?
C'est tout.	That's all.
C'est (trop) cher.	It's (too) expensive.
Je vais le/la prendre! (**le** for a masculine item, **la** for feminine)	I'll take it!
Je vais les prendre.	I'll take them.

à la poste — ***at the post office***

la boîte aux lettres	postbox
la carte	postcard
la lettre	letter

Useful phrases

Je voudrais	I'd like
… un timbre pour l'Angleterre	… a stamp for England
… une télécarte	… a phone card
… envoyer une carte en Angleterre	… to send a card to England
Où est la boîte aux lettres?	Where's the postbox?

SEE ALSO Food

Snacks

une crêpe	*pancake*
un croque-monsieur	*toasted cheese and ham sandwich*
une glace	*ice cream*
une portion de frites	*portion of chips*
un sandwich (au jambon)	*(ham) sandwich*
un sandwich (au fromage)	*(cheese) sandwich*

SEE ALSO Drinks, Food, Partitive article

Sports

Tu aimes le sport? *Do you like sport?*

Oui, j'aime… *Yes, I like…*

l'athlétisme (m.)	*athletics*	la natation	*swimming*
le basket	*basketball*	le patin à roulettes	*roller-skating*
le cricket	*cricket*	le patinage	*ice-skating*
le cyclisme	*cycling*	le rugby	*rugby*
l'équitation (f.)	*horseriding*	le ski	*skiing*
le foot	*football*	le tennis	*tennis*
la gymnastique	*gymnastics*	la voile	*sailing*

Note that when you say you play some sports, you use **je fais** (from the verb **faire** – *to do/to make*) and for other sports **je joue** (from the verb **jouer** – *to play*). Look at these examples.

Je fais du cyclisme/du vélo.
Je fais de l'équitation.
Je fais de la gymnastique.
Je fais de la natation.
Je joue au basket.
Je joue au cricket.
Je joue au foot.
Je joue au rugby.
Je joue au tennis.

SEE ALSO Free time – going out

Television

Qu'est-ce que tu aimes (regarder) à la télévision?
What do you like (watching) on TV?

la causerie	*chat show*
le dessin animé	*cartoon*
le documentaire	*documentary*
le feuilleton	*serial/soap*
les films (m.pl.)	*films*
les informations (f.pl.) } le journal télévisé	*news*
les jeux (m.pl.)	*game shows*
la météo	*weather forecast*
la pièce de théâtre	*play*
le sport	*sport*
les variétés (f.pl.)	*variety show*

SEE ALSO Cinema

Time

Quelle heure est-il?	*What time is it?*
Il est une heure.	*It's one o'clock.*
Il est deux heures.	*It's two o'clock.*
Il est midi.	*It's midday.*
Il est minuit.	*It's midnight.*

Time 'past' the hour

Il est deux heures cinq.	*It's five past two.*
Il est trois heures dix.	*It's ten past three.*
Il est quatre heures et quart.	*It's quarter past four.*
Il est cinq heures vingt.	*It's twenty past five.*
Il est six heures et demie.	*It's half past six.*
Il est midi/minuit et demi.	*It's half past twelve (midday/midnight).*

Note that with **midi/minuit**, there is no **e** at the end of **demi**.

Time 'to' the hour

Il est sept heures moins vingt-cinq.	*It's twenty-five to seven.*
Il est huit heures moins vingt.	*It's twenty to eight.*
Il est neuf heures moins le quart.	*It's quarter to nine.*
Il est dix heures moins dix.	*It's ten to ten.*
Il est onze heures moins cinq.	*It's five to eleven.*

The 24-hour clock

The 24-hour clock is often used on timetables, signs, notices, etc.

20h30	(8.30 p.m.)	vingt heures trente
20h40	(8.40 p.m.)	vingt heures quarante

EXAM TIP

Do not use *et quart*, *et demie* or *moins le quart* with the 24-hour clock.

42

Town – la ville

l'aéroport (m.)	airport
l'agence de voyages (f.)	travel agent's
la banque	bank
le bâtiment	building
la bibliothèque	library
le bureau	office
la cathédrale	cathedral
le centre commercial	shopping centre
le château	castle
le cinéma	cinema
le commissariat	police station
l'église (f.)	church
la gare	station
la gare routière	coach station
la gendarmerie	police station
l'hôpital (m.)	hospital
l'hôtel de ville (m.) } la mairie	town hall
le jardin public	park
le musée	museum
la poste	post office
le stade	sports stadium
la station-service	petrol station
le théâtre	theatre

Transport

l'autobus/le bus	*bus*	le train	*train*
l'avion (m.)	*plane*	le TGV (train à	*express train*
le bateau	*boat*	grande vitesse)	
le camion	*lorry*	la traversée	*crossing*
le car	*coach*	le vélo	*bike*
le ferry	*ferry*	le vélomoteur	*moped*
l'hélicoptère (m.)	*helicopter*	le VTT (vélo	*mountain bike*
le métro	*underground/*	tout terrain)	
	tube/metro	la voiture	*car*
la moto	*motorbike*	le vol	*flight*
à pied	*on foot*		

Note: Je voyage **en** train/**en** bus, etc.   *I travel by train/bus, etc.*
But:
Je voyage **à** pied/**à** cheval.   *I travel on foot/on horseback.*

Buying a train ticket

Je voudrais…	*I'd like…*
un billet ⎫	*a ticket*
un ticket ⎭	
un aller-simple	*single*
un aller-retour	*return ticket*
première classe	*first class*
en deuxième classe	*in second class*
le guichet	*ticket office*
le tarif réduit	*reduced rate*
À quelle heure part le prochain train?	*When does the next train leave?*
C'est quel quai?	*Which platform is it?*
À quelle heure arrive le train?	*When does the train arrive?*
Je voudrais réserver une place.	*I'd like to reserve a seat.*
Je voudrais un aller-simple à Paris, s'il vous plaît.	*I'd like a single ticket to Paris, please.*

Other useful transport phrases

Où est l'arrêt de bus?	*Where is the bus stop?*
N'oubliez pas de composter votre billet.	*Don't forget to stamp your ticket.*
le buffet	*buffet restaurant*
la consigne	*left-luggage office*
C'est bien le car pour Dijon?	*Is this the right coach for Dijon?*

Verbs

Verbs say what is happening – they are words of action or 'doing' words. In the dictionary, you will find verbs listed under their infinitives – their names. The equivalent of this in English is *to* + action, e.g. *to swim*, *to run*, etc.

All verbs in French end in **er**, **ir** or **re**, e.g. **manger** (*to eat*), **finir** (*to finish*), **vendre** (*to sell*). There are two types of verbs: regular and irregular. Regular verbs follow a set pattern, but irregular ones don't.

You can't use the infinitive with the subject of the verb (**je**, **tu**, etc.). You need to change the verb according to who is doing the action, e.g. **je mange** *(I eat)*, **nous mangeons** (*we eat*). The end of the verb changes for different people.

Tense of verbs

At this stage in your learning, you need to be able to use verbs in different time zones – past, present and future.

SEE ALSO Future tense (near future), Negatives, Past (perfect) tense, Present tense, Reflexive verbs

Weather – la météo

Quel temps fait-il?	What's the weather like?
Il fait beau.	*It's fine.*
Il fait chaud.	*It's hot.*
Il fait froid.	*It's cold.*
Il fait mauvais.	*The weather is bad.*
Il fait 25°.	*It is 25°.*
Il fait du brouillard.	*It's foggy.*
Il fait du vent.	*It's windy.*
Il y a de l'orage.	*It's stormy.*
Il gèle.	*It's freezing.*
Il y a/Il fait du soleil.	*It's sunny.*
Il neige.	*It's snowing.*
Il pleut.	*It's raining.*

To describe the weather in the past, use the following phrases.

Il faisait instead of **Il fait**.

e.g. Il faisait chaud.	*It was hot.*

Il y avait instead of **Il y a**.

e.g. Il y avait du vent.	*It was windy.*

Il neigeait.	*It was snowing.*
Il pleuvait.	*It was raining.*

Work   see Jobs